ARTIST TRANSCRIPTIONS PIANO

THE BILL CHARLAP COLLECTION

Cover photo by Donald Dietz

ISBN 978-0-634-06743 3

HAL•LEONARD®
CORPORATION

7777 W. BLUEMOUND RD. P.O. BOX 13819 MILWAUKEE, WI 53213

Visit Hal Leonard Online at
www.halleonard.com

BIOGRAPHY

One of the world's premier jazz pianists, Bill Charlap has performed and recorded with many leading artists of our time, ranging from jazz masters Phil Woods and Wynton Marsalis to singers Tony Bennett and Barbra Streisand. Since 1997, he has led the Bill Charlap Trio with bassist Peter Washington and drummer Kenny Washington, now recognized as one of the leading groups in jazz. Charlap is the artistic director of New York City's Jazz in July Festival at the 92nd Street Y, and he has produced concerts for Jazz at Lincoln Center, the JVC Jazz Festival and the Hollywood Bowl. A two-time Grammy nominee, Charlap is married to renowned jazz pianist Renee Rosnes, and the two often collaborate in a duo piano setting. In the sping of 2010,   Charlap and Rosnes will release *Double Portrait*, a duo piano recording on the Blue Note label.

The Best Thing for You

from the Stage Production *CALL ME MADAM*

Words and Music by Irving Berlin

All Through the Night (Criss Cross 1153)

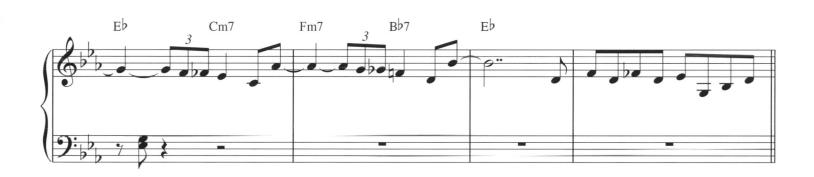

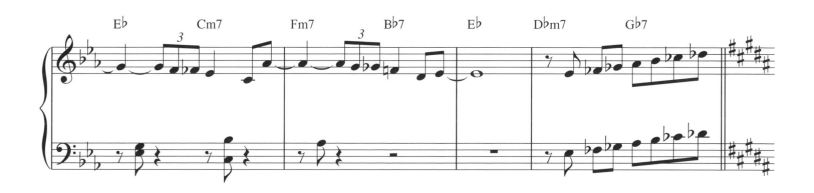

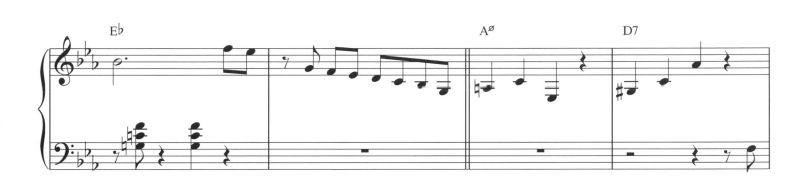

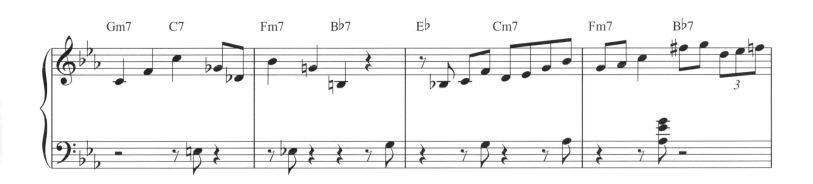

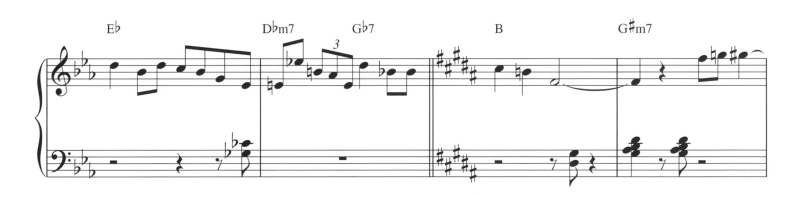

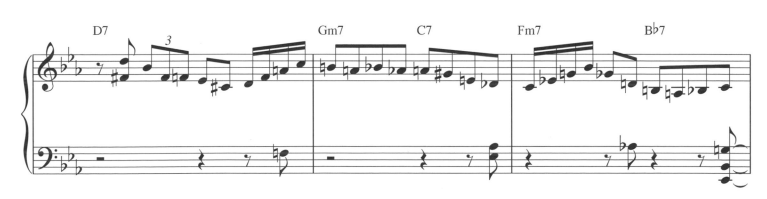

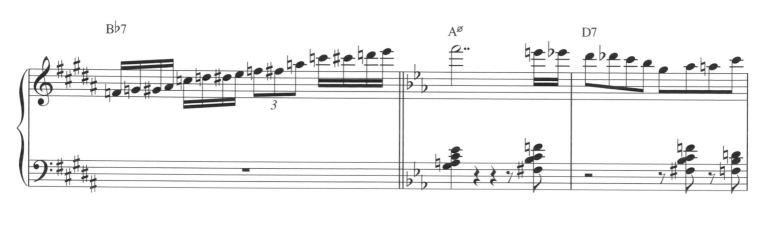

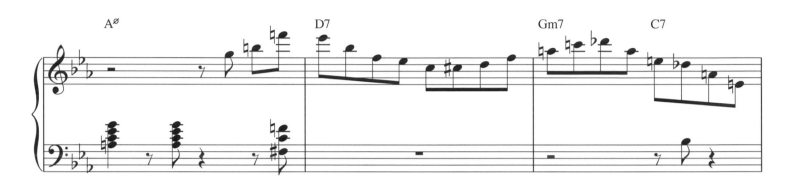

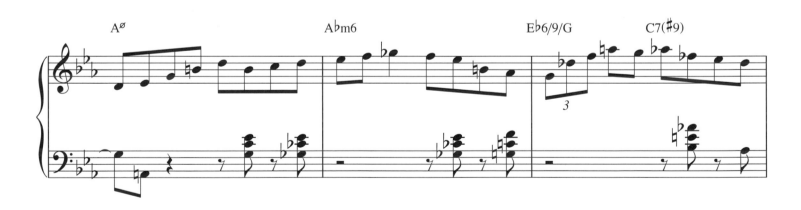

11

I Walk with Music

Words and Music by Hoagy Carmichael and Johnny Mercer
Stardust (Blue Note 35985)

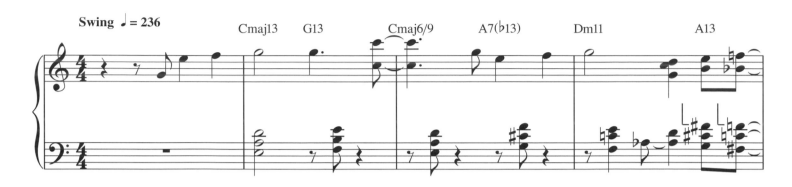

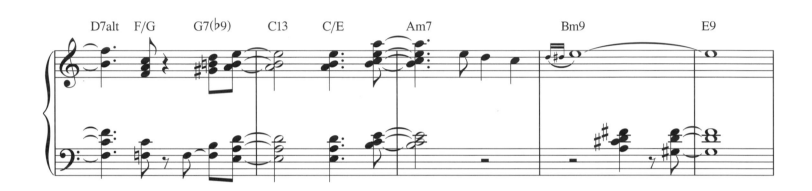

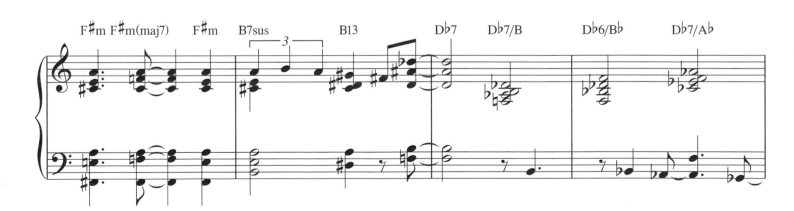

15

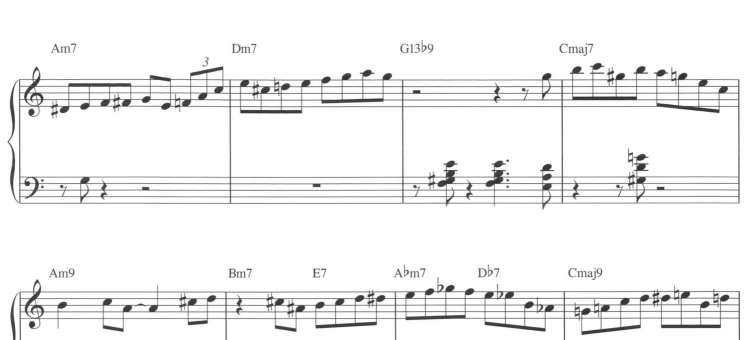

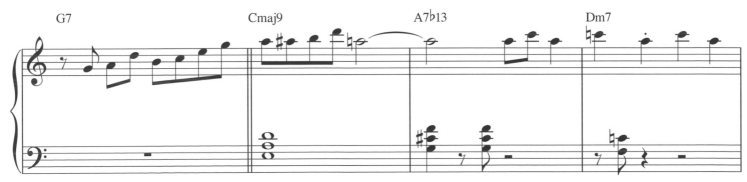

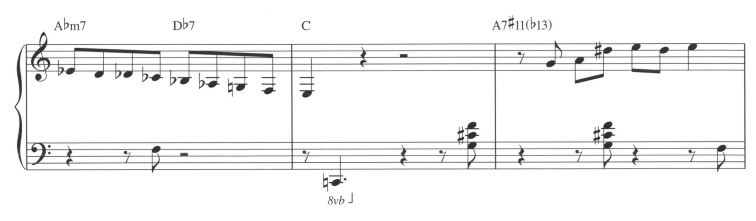

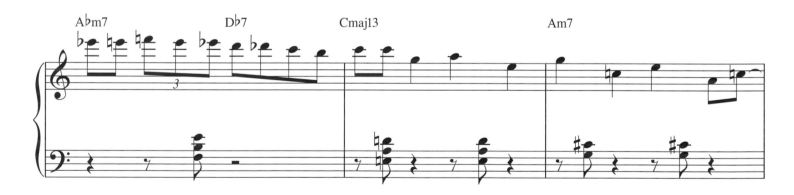

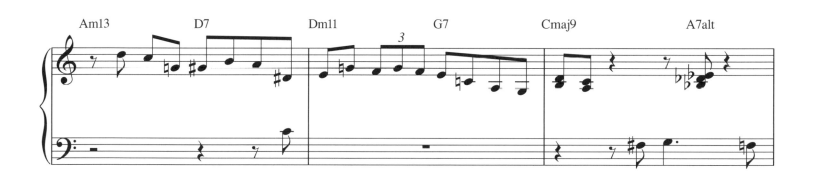

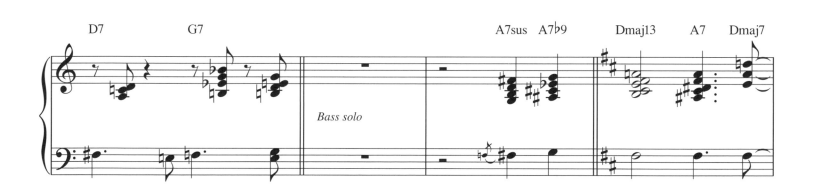

In the Still of the Night

Words and Music by Cole Porter

Written in the Stars (Blue Note 27291)

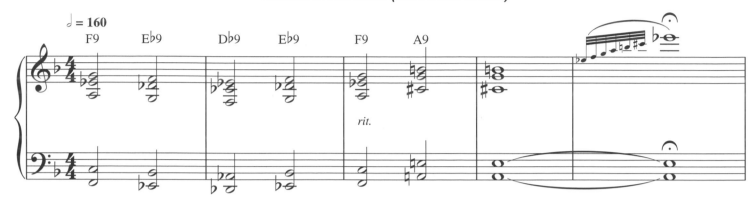

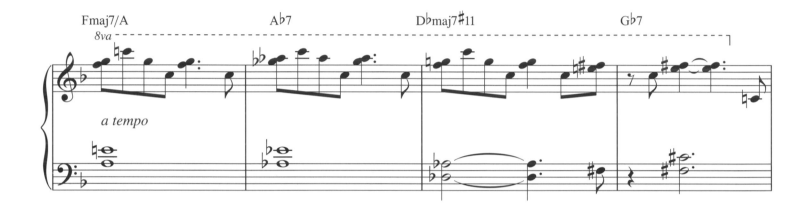

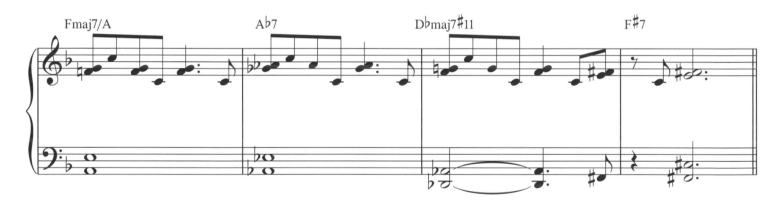

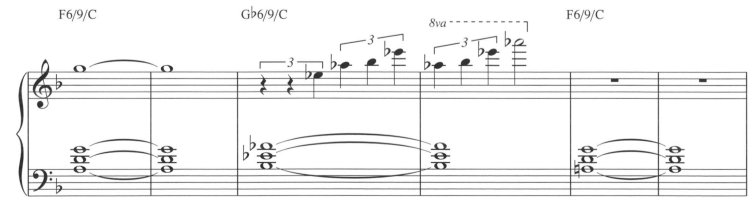

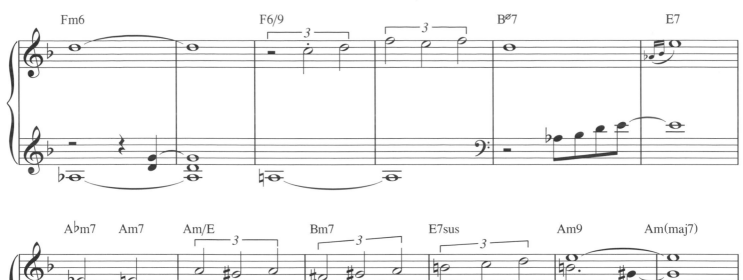

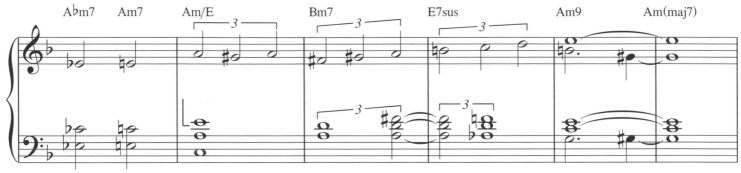

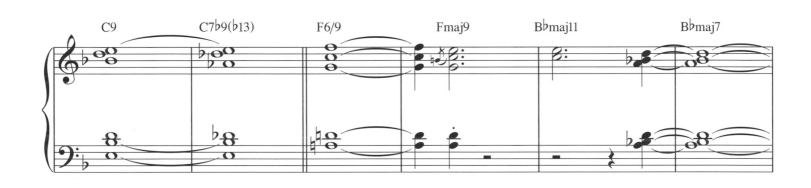

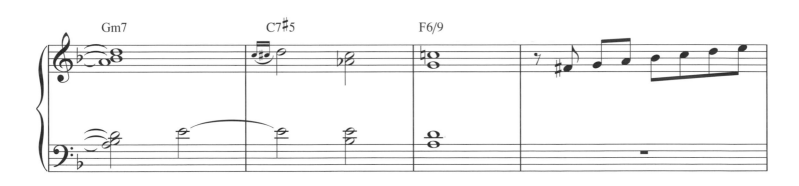

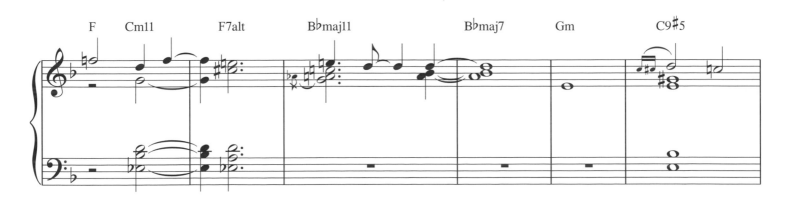

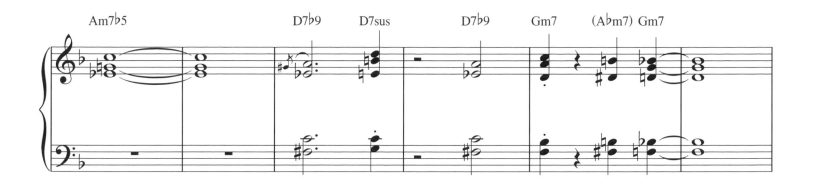

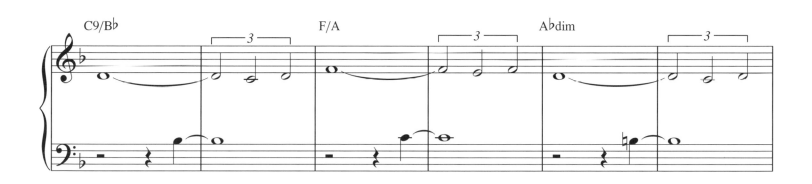

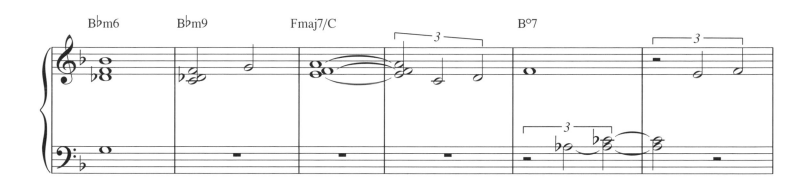

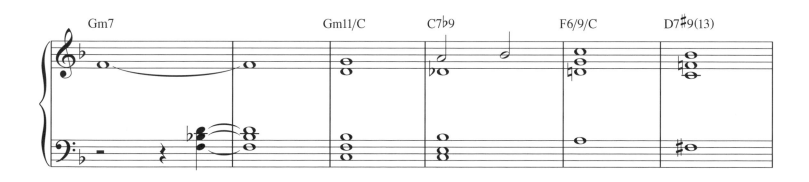

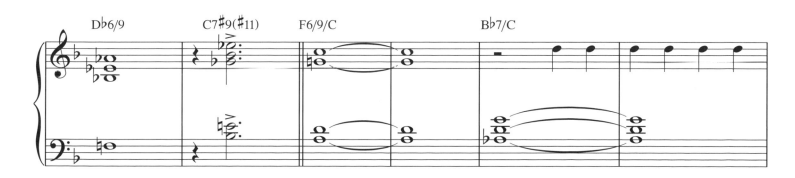

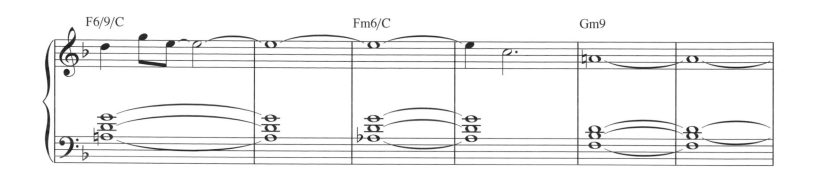

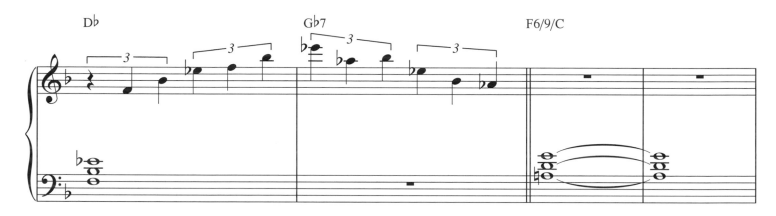

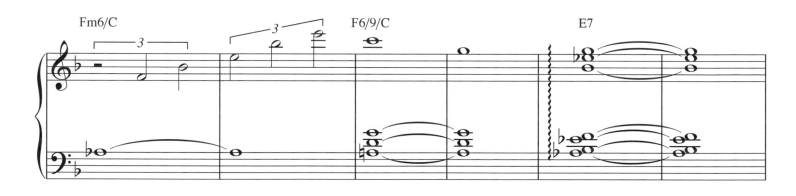

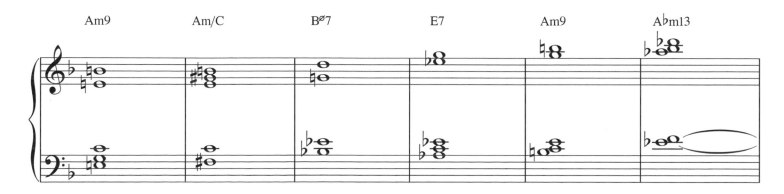

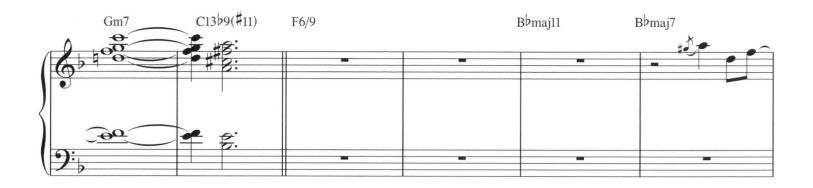

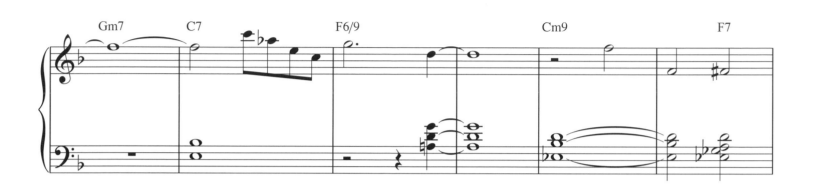

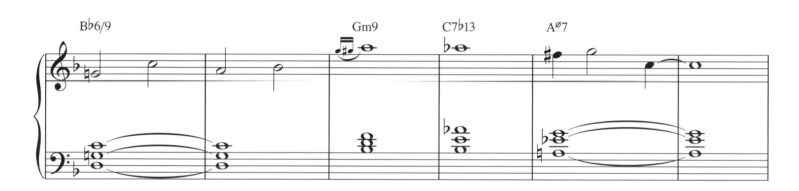

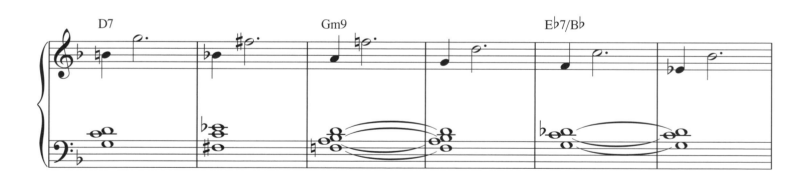

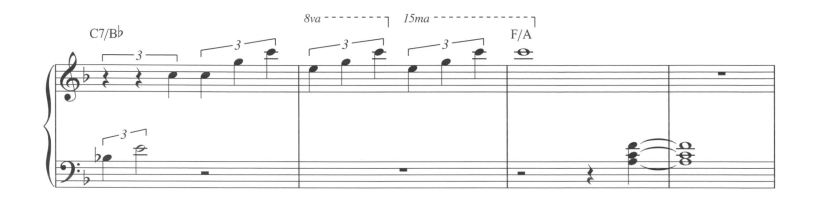

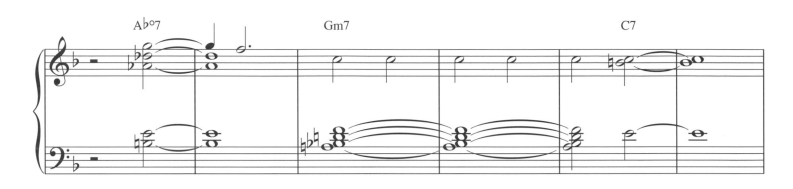

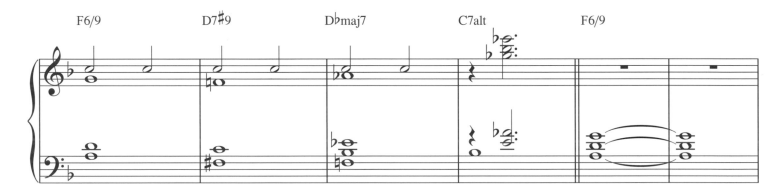

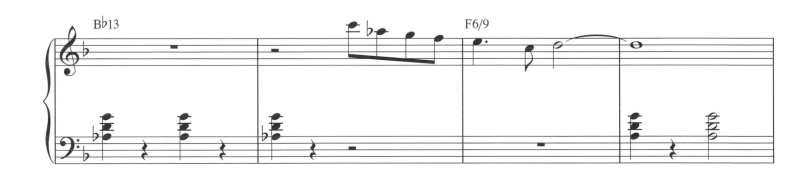

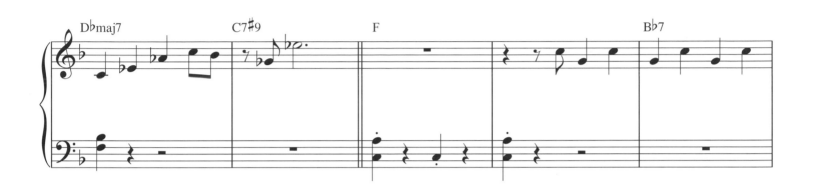

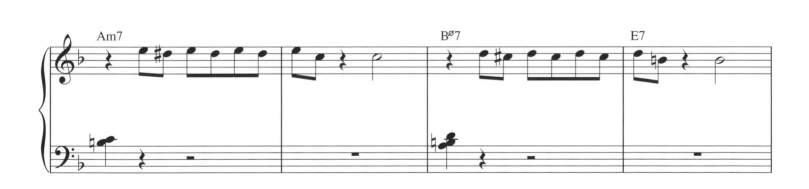

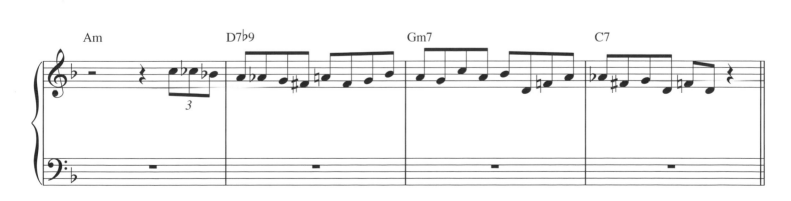

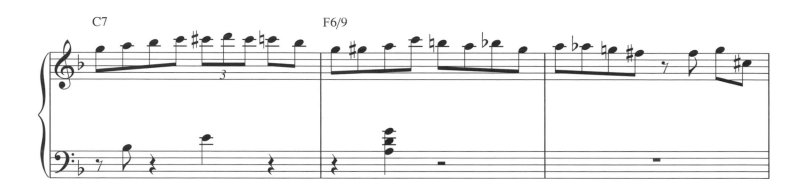

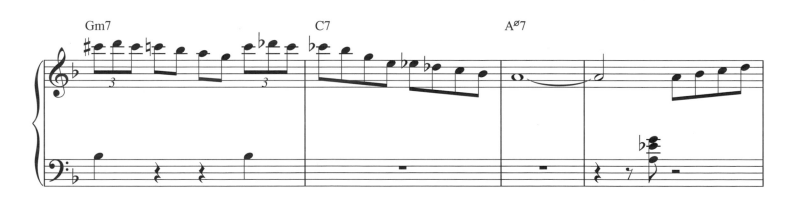

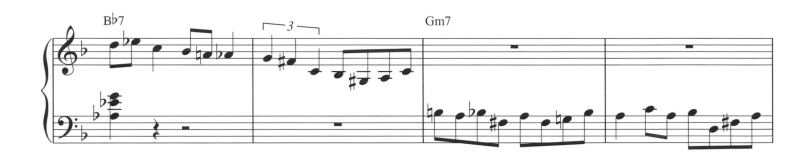

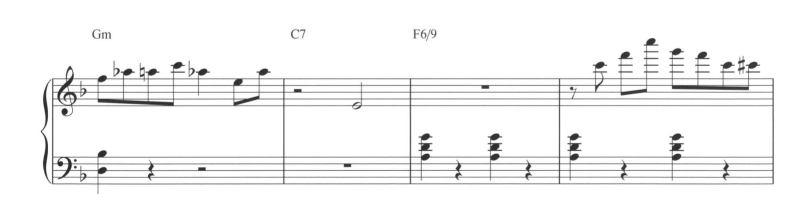

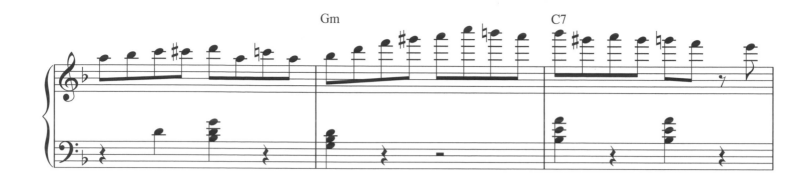

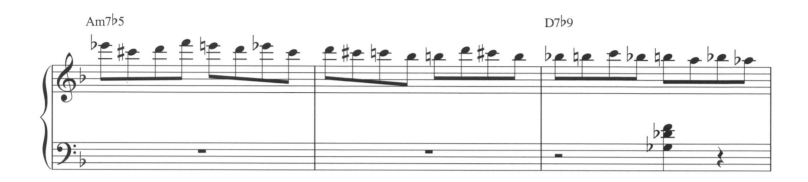

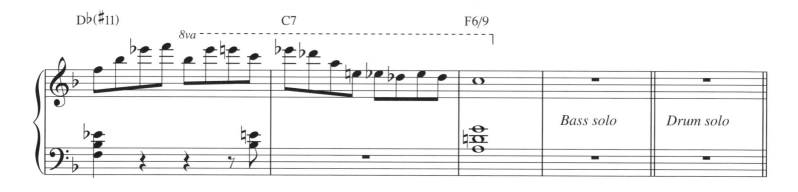

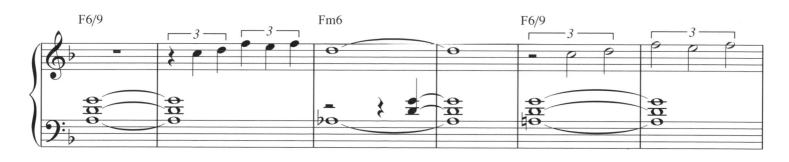

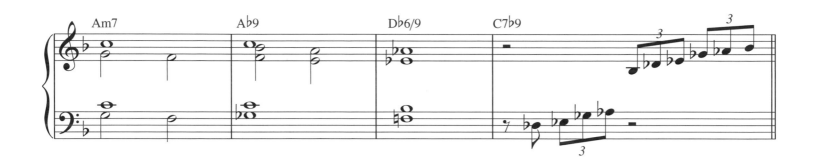

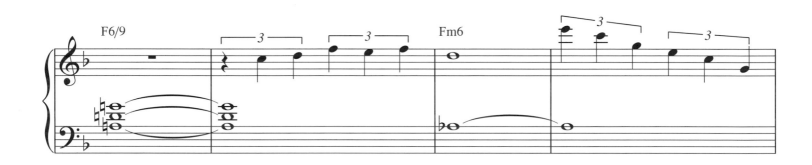

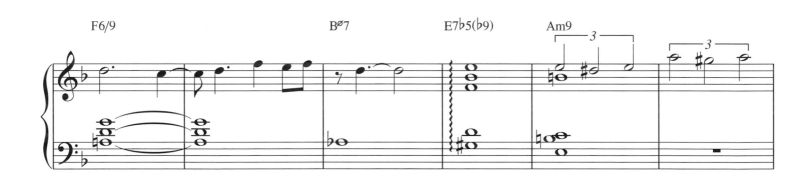

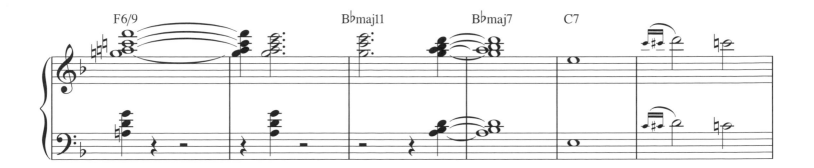

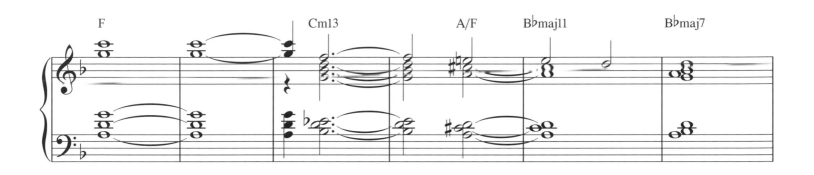

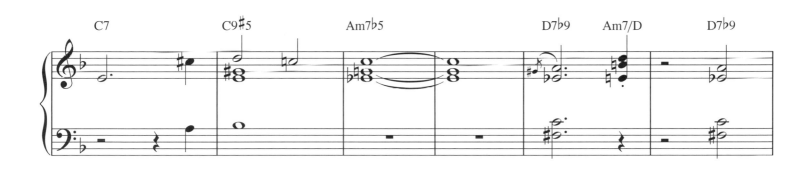

It Was Written in the Stars

Lyric by Leo Robin
Music by Harold Arlen
Written in the Stars (Blue Note 27291)

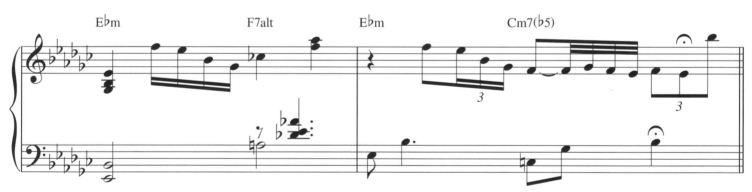

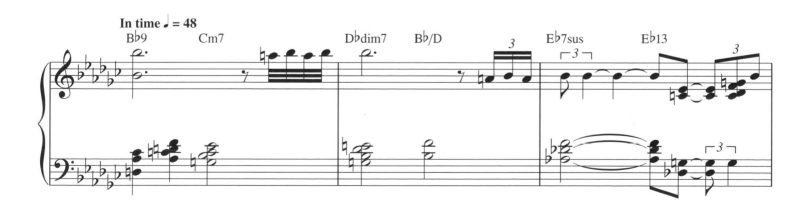

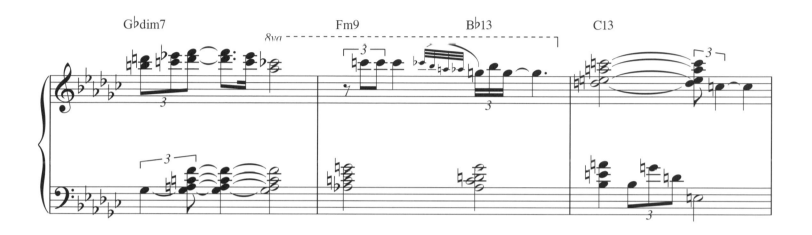

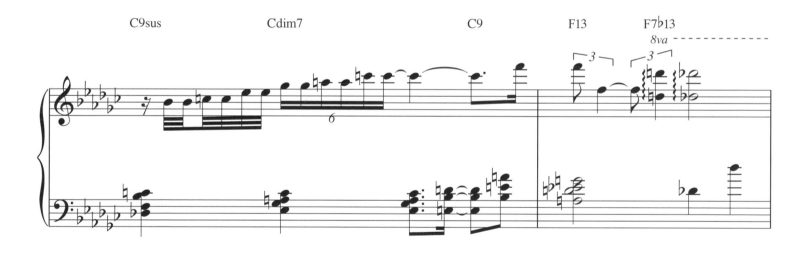

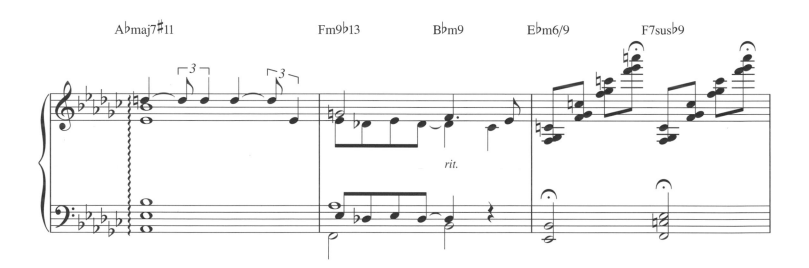

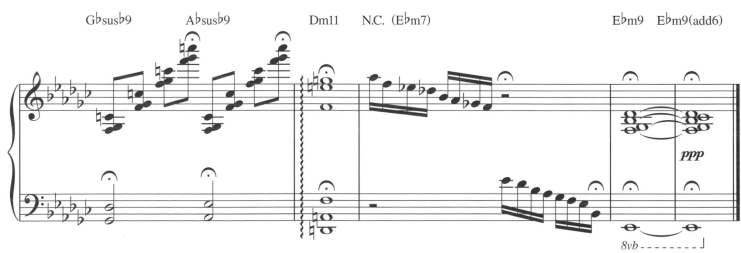

It's So Peaceful in the Country

Words and Music by Alec Wilder

All Through the Night (Criss Cross 1153)

54

56

Jubilee

Words by Stanley Adams
Music by Hoagy Carmichael and Stanley Adams
Stardust (Blue Note 35985)

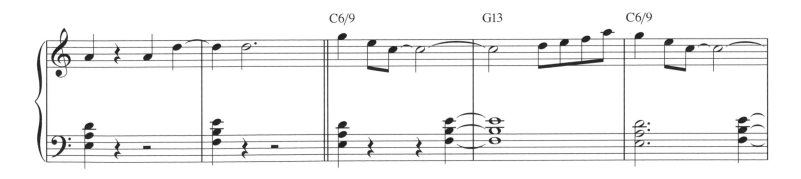

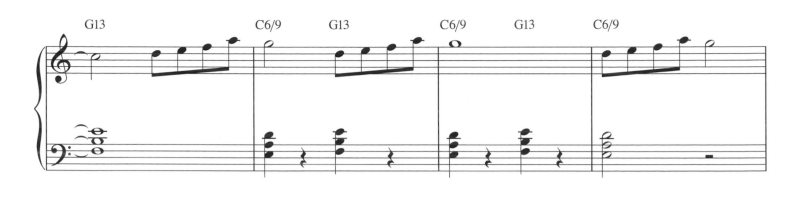

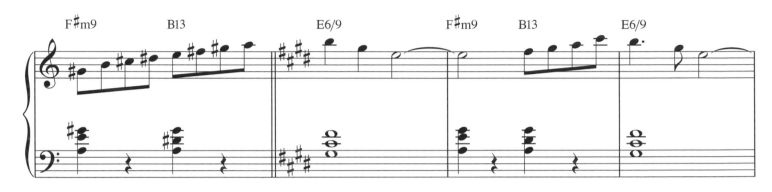

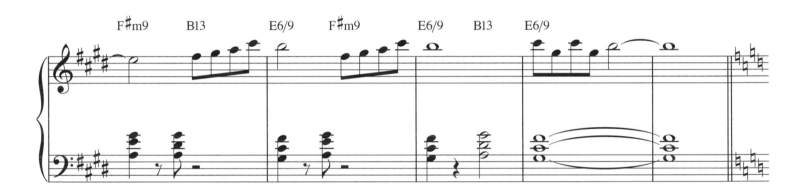

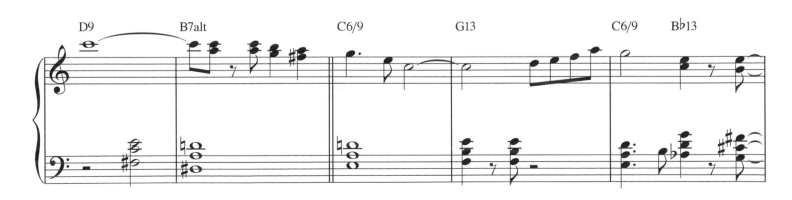

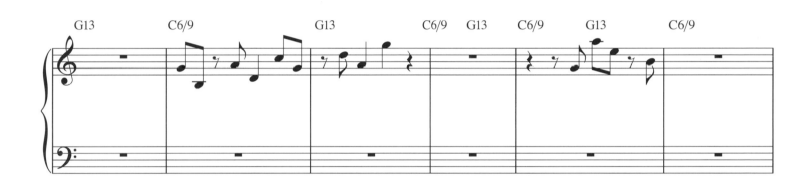

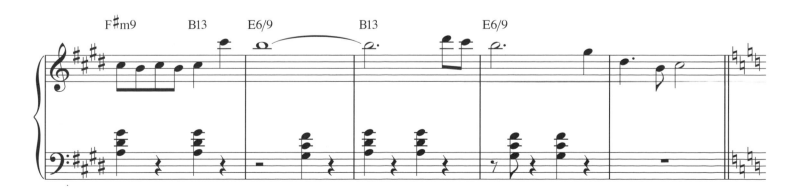

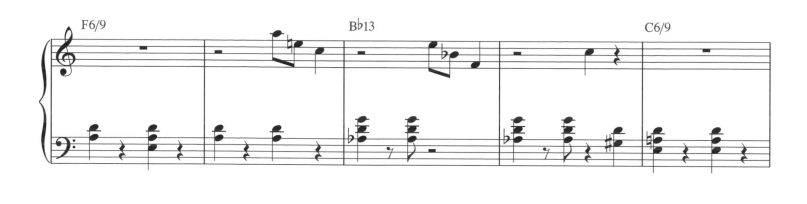

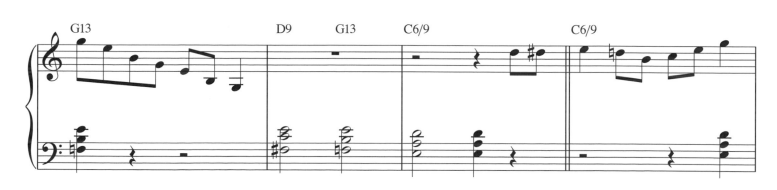

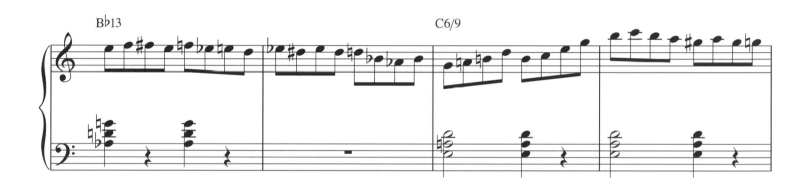

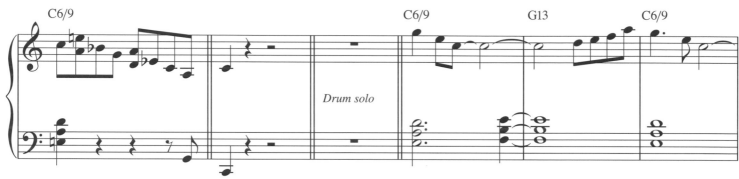

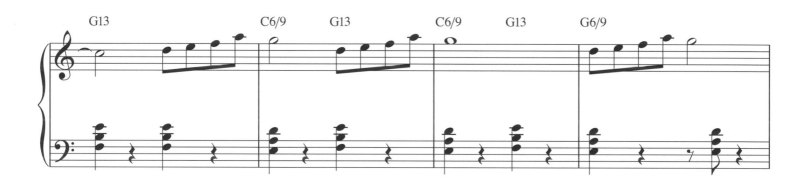

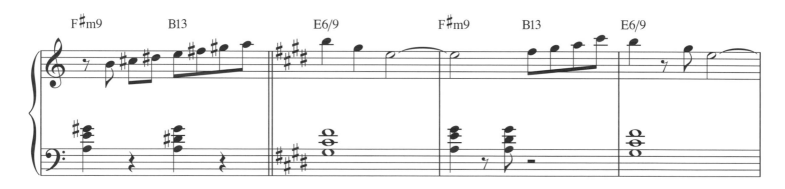

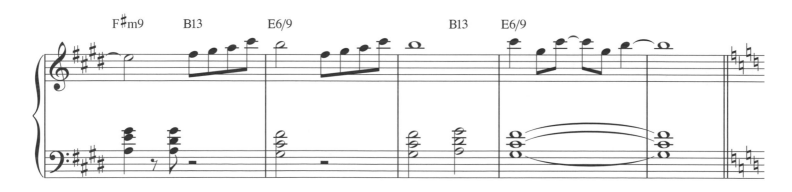

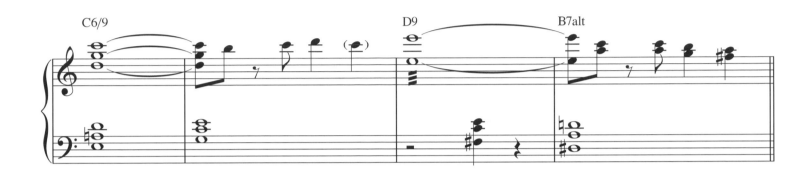

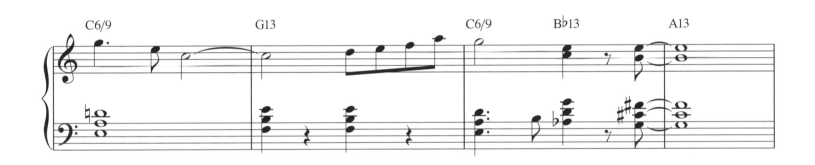

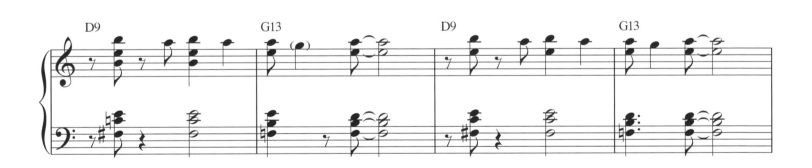

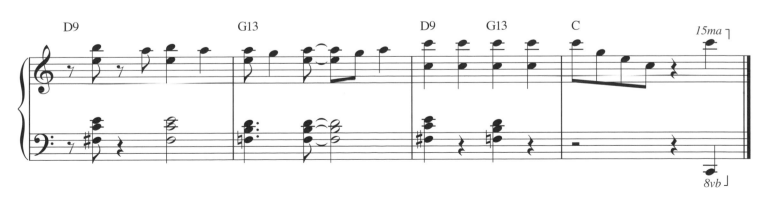

The Man That Got Away

Lyric by Ira Gershwin
Music by Harold Arlen
Written in the Stars (Blue Note 27291)

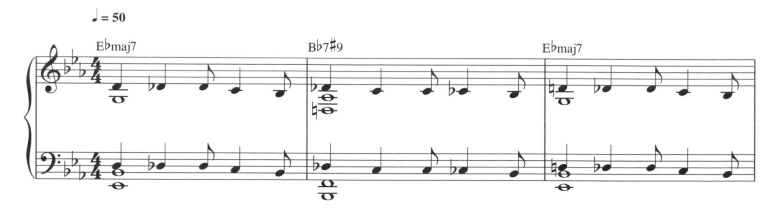

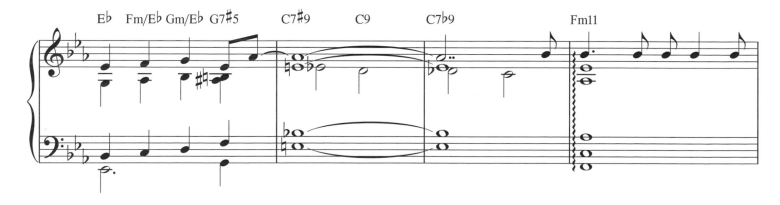

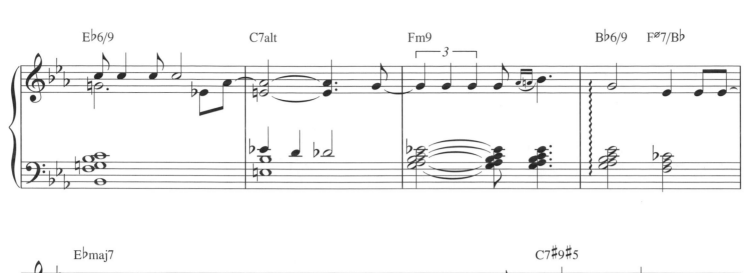

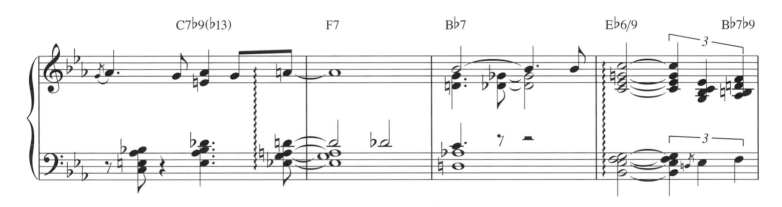

On a Slow Boat to China

By Frank Loesser

Written in the Stars (Blue Note 27291)

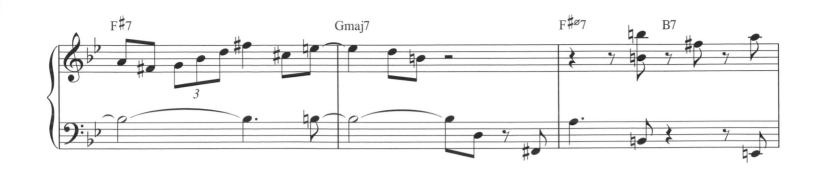

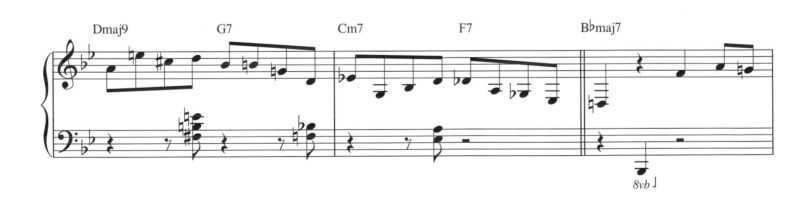

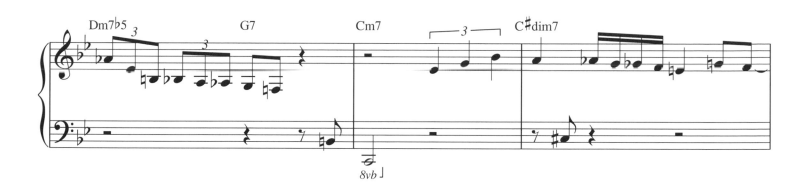

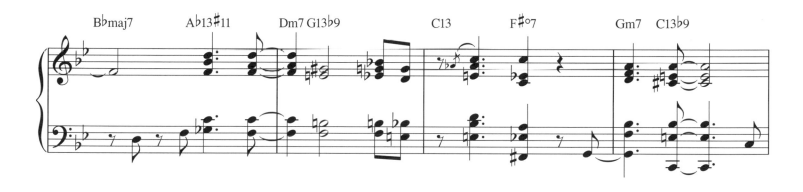

One for My Baby
(And One More for the Road)

Lyric by Johnny Mercer
Music by Harold Arlen
Written in the Stars (Blue Note 27291)

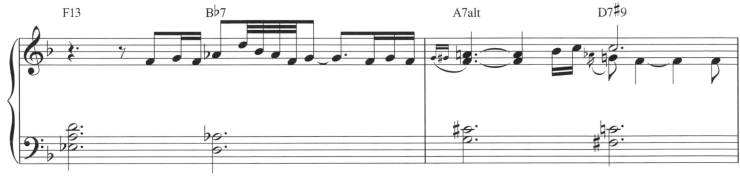

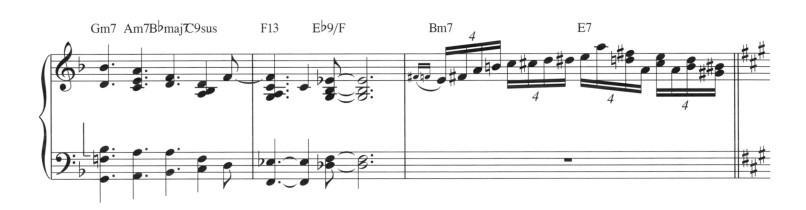

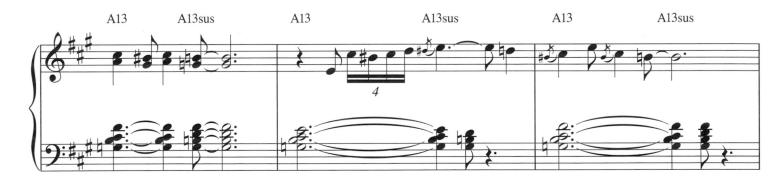

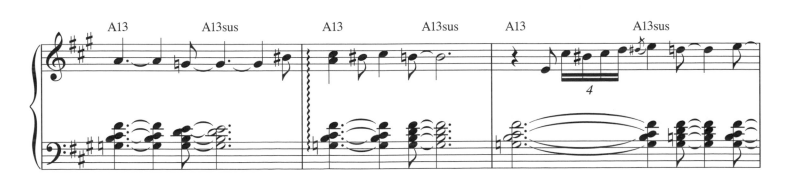

Skylark

Words by Johnny Mercer
Music by Hoagy Carmichael
Stardust (Blue Note 35985)

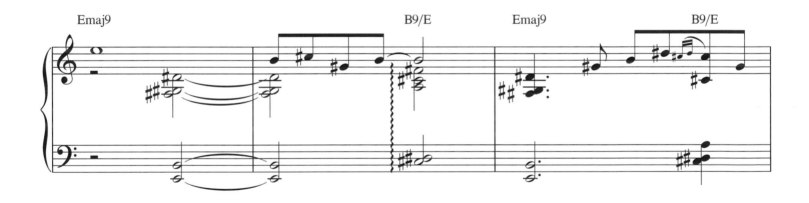